IN SEARCH OF PEACE

SONALI CHAUDHARY

For the readers,

who all make the dream come true ...

Contents

Foreword

It was the first time when I had felt that these statements has matched the situation of life.

The author has written the poem in a very simple and authentic way that could be easily understood by everyone. A diamond is a non metal still its shine make it different from others. In the same way, every word of the poem used by the author is simple and easy but the emotion which come at random according to the phase of the life make it more attractive.

To share the personal experience with all the readers make a clear vision about the author and its perspective for writting it.

Sonali

Preface

Sometimes most of the adventure, we feel cannot get recorded by the technology but our mind, can capture it for the lifetime. Everyone may have experience almost the same way of life but to express it with other with a special route make it diffterent. The main focus of writting it is to spread the idea of life practice. In this book, I have shared my experience and also how it all changed me .

1. Fear of Loosing

Hands are too freeze
It's so shocking
Pleasant turns to a horrific breeze.
The whole world has colourful light
can see everything
Still life is a dark night.
A pumping sound is near
there is nothing
Yet a loosing fear.
Staring at one without blinking
became speechless person
to the tough thinking .
Temperature is not raised
However there is a fever
That's why I locked myself into a cage.

2. Set to free

Forget to take a flight
instead of her
Life is far better of a kite.
The prison is full of fear
Remembering those preety moments
Ages are passing through tear.
Oh majesty! let her life free
try to think twice
they look only good on a tree.
Smashed the tied up tracker
All emotions burstout
Finally burnt the freedom cracker.
Streching the face to smile
to feel fresh air
which was far a mile.
The water, the food are change
however glad to see
since crossed all the seal range.

3. Sound of peace

The moon appears to be bright
mile away standing on a place
In the silent midnight.
Sea seems so silent
Apart from one
As the waves look violent.
Groups of ant move in a queue
looking too large with small
give me a goosebump view.
The wind is blowing
Seeing this nature's beauty
The stars start glowing.

4. Puzzle

Showing their will
to make a long fly,
Dreams became fulfil
when move to high sky.
Reality is too far
as you are not sucessfull
till you have a big car.

5. Self Doubt

Never doubt on your own thinking
When other say something,
Because they want your mind to be kinking
So always be one thing either nothing.
Never mind anyone's word
when it is not the truth,
Be like a flying bird
who is enjoying their youth.
Life has many situation
Trust is one of them
where some do or some blame
This is what the magic of creation.

6. Rain

Hardest time is to suffer
just you've to be tough and tougher.
Have to wet in this rain
Because not definite how much it pain.
Hurt is not the worry
just not do anything in hurry.
Everything will be fine
if everyone will say this pain is mine.

7. Filled blank

One who gives everything in free
also known as charity tree.
No love, no respect to them
which they are,
Always do some blame
Yet love is too far.

Heartful Note

Every poem has a deep and a profound meaning amd I am leaving upto all my readers to take it the way they want. The journey that had been explained has passed out from all of us but in a differrent plot. The title of the book " In search of peace " states that it doesn't matter whether your words are simple or compex what matter is how you express your feelings about life. The last poem ' Filled blank' bears a special palce in my heart. There are mysteries left inside all the lines of the poem which I want make you to solve.